The Super Easy

Anti-Inflammatory

Diet Cookbook

100, Quick, Easy & Quick Nutritional Recipes, 7-Days Meal Plans to Soothe Your Immune System and Balance Your Body

Serena Kafta

The Super Easy
Anti-Inflammatory
Diet Cookbook

100, Quick, Easy & Quick Nutritional Recipes, 7-Days Meal
Plans to Soothe Your Immune System and Balance Your Body

Serena Kafta

Copyright Page

Table of Contents

Introduction

The anti-inflammatory diet has gained popularity in recent years as something of a panacea to modern living. Eating a diet rich in added sugars, refined carbs and processed and packaged foods, drinking alcohol, prolonged stress and a lack of exercise are all lifestyle factors that can promote inflammation in the body, so switching to an anti-inflammatory diet may help.

However, in small amounts, inflammation can be a good thing. 'Acute' inflammation is the cornerstone of the immune system's healing response, and without it, we wouldn't recover from infection, illness or injury. But when inflammation persists over weeks, months, or years, becoming 'chronic', it can be hazardous to your health. So how can you ensure you get the right balance and avoid tipping into dangerous inflammation territory without denying your body what it needs?

Certain foods can help to reduce or even prevent chronic inflammation, known as the anti-inflammatory diet. We spoke to Dr Sarah Brewer, medical director at Healthspan, about which specific foods influence the inflammation process and where to start with the anti-inflammatory diet:

What is inflammation?

Inflammation is your body's way of fighting against infections, injuries, and toxins in an attempt to heal itself. 'Acute inflammation is the type that comes on quickly,' says Dr Brewer. 'The affected part becomes red, hot, swollen, painful and unable to function properly.' Your immune system reacts by sending antibodies, proteins and extra blood to the site of the issue, usually for a few hours or days until the healing process is complete.

However, sometimes inflammation is chronic, which means it lingers. This is due to the presence of a type of scavenger cell called a macrophage, says Dr Brewer, which releases powerful chemicals, including free radicals. Chronic inflammation may be caused by:

- A medical condition that causes the immune system to malfunction.
- Long-term exposure to irritants, such as industrial chemicals or air pollutants.
- Lifestyle factors, such as smoking, obesity, alcohol, stress and diet.

Left unchecked, chronic inflammation acts on your tissues and organs. 'It occurs throughout the body and especially affects the circulation,' Dr Brewer says. 'You won't feel any soreness or see any swelling, but the immune cells and chemicals present can cause slow damage that increases the risk of type 2 diabetes, heart attack and stroke.'

For that reason, chronic inflammation is linked to a host of health issues and diseases, including inflammatory bowel disease, asthma, rheumatoid arthritis and cancer. This type of inflammation can be assessed by measuring blood levels of CRP (C-reactive protein) in the blood.

13 Ways Inflammation Can Affect Your Health

1. It Fights Infection

Inflammation is most visible (and most beneficial) when it's helping to repair a wound or fight off an illness.

"You've noticed your body's inflammatory response if you've ever had a fever or a sore throat with swollen glands," says Timothy Denning, PhD, prior associate professor and immunology researcher at Georgia State University, or an infected cut that's become red and warm to the touch.

The swelling, redness, and warmth are signs that your immune system is sending white blood cells, immune cell-stimulating growth factors, and nutrients to the affected areas. In this sense, inflammation is a healthy and necessary function for healing. But this type of helpful inflammation is only temporary: when the infection or illness is gone, inflammation should go away as well.

2. It Prepares You for Battles

Another type of inflammation occurs in response to emotional stress. Instead of blood cells rushing to one part of the body, however, inflammatory markers called C-reactive proteins are released into the blood stream and travel throughout the body.

This is the body's biological response to impending danger—a "flight or fight" response that floods you with adrenaline and could help you escape a life-threatening situation. But unrelenting stress over a long period of time—or dwelling on past stressful events—can cause C-reactive protein levels to be constantly elevated, which can be a factor in many chronic health conditions, like those on the following slides.

3. It Can Harm Your Gut

"Many of the body's immune cells cluster around the intestines," says Denning. Most of the time, those immune cells ignore the trillions of healthy bacteria that live in the gut. "But for some people, that tolerance seems to be broken," says Denning, "and their immune cells begin to react to the bacteria, creating chronic inflammation."

The immune cells can attack the digestive tract itself, an autoimmune condition known as inflammatory bowel disease (IBD), which includes ulcerative colitis and Crohn's disease. The symptoms include diarrhea, cramps, ulcers, and may even require surgical removal of the intestines. Doctors aren't exactly sure why some people get IBD, but genetics, environment, antibiotics, diet, and stress management all seem to play a role.

4. It Can Harm Your Joints

When inflammation occurs in the joints, it's can cause serious damage. One joint-damaging condition is rheumatoid arthritis (RA)—another example of an autoimmune disorder that appears to have a genetic component but is also linked to smoking, a lack of vitamin D, and other risk factors. A 2013 Yale University study, for example, found that a salty diet may contribute to the development of RA.

People with RA experience pain and stiffness in their inflamed joints. But because the immune reaction isn't limited to the joints, says Denning, they're also at higher risk for problems with their eyes and other body parts.

Psoriatic arthritis also involves inflammation in the joints, and its symptoms are similar to those of RA. But in addition to painful, stiff joints, people with PsA may also experience changes in the nails, like pitting. Most people with psoriatic arthritis first develop psoriasis, another autoimmune condition, on their skin. Around 30% of people with psoriasis are thought to develop psoriatic arthritis, and you may be more likely to do so if your skin psoriasis affects your nails.

5. It's Linked to Heart Disease

Any part of your body that's been injured or damaged can trigger inflammation, even the insides of blood vessels. The formation of fatty plaque in the arteries can trigger chronic inflammation. The fatty plaques attract white blood cells, grow larger, and can form blood clots, which can cause a heart attack. One specific protein, called interleukin-6 (IL-6), may play a key role, according to a 2012 study published in The Lancet.

Obesity and unhealthy eating increases inflammation in the body, but even otherwise healthy people who experience chronic inflammation because of an autoimmune disorder such as rheumatoid arthritis, psoriasis, or celiac disease appear to have a higher risk of heart disease, regardless of their weight or eating habits.

6. It's Linked to a Higher Risk of Cancer

With so much noise surrounding possible causes of cancer (underwire bras, seriously?), it's hard to determine what the true dangers are. The good news is that when it comes to food, there aren't that many specific types linked to cancer.

7. It May Sabotage Your Sleep

Insufficient sleep is linked to a host of health problems, from depression to cardiovascular disease. Make sure you're falling asleep quickly so you can get a good night's rest. Watch this video for six simple tricks to avoid insomnia.

8. It's Bad for Your Lungs

When inflammation occurs in the lungs, it can cause fluid accumulation and narrowing of the airways, making it difficult to breathe. Infections, asthma, and chronic obstructive pulmonary disease (COPD) (which includes emphysema and chronic bronchitis) are all characterized by inflammation in the lungs.

Smoking, exposure to air pollution or household chemicals, being overweight, and even consumption of cured meats have been linked to lung inflammation.

9. It Damages Gums

Inflammation can also wreak havoc on your mouth in the form of periodontitis, a chronic inflammation of the gums caused by bacteria accumulation. This disease causes gums to recede and the skeletal structure around the teeth become weakened or damaged. Brushing and flossing regularly can prevent periodontitis, and one 2010 Harvard University study found that eating anti-inflammatory omega-3 fatty acids (such as fish or fish oil) may also help.

Periodontal disease doesn't just affect oral health, either. Studies show that inflammation of the gums is linked to heart disease and dementia as well, since bacteria in the mouth may also trigger inflammation elsewhere in the body.

10. It Makes Weight Loss More Difficult

Obesity is a major cause of inflammation in the body, and losing weight is one of the most effective ways to fight it. But that's sometimes easier said than done, because elevated levels of inflammation-related proteins can also make weight loss more difficult than it should be.

For starters, chronic inflammation can influence hunger signals and slow down metabolism, so you eat more and burn fewer calories. Inflammation can also increase insulin resistance (which raises your risk for diabetes) and has been linked with future weight gain.

11. It Damages Bones

Inflammation throughout the body can interfere with bone growth and even promote increased bone loss, according to a 2009 review study published in the Journal of Endocrinology. Researchers suspect that inflammatory markers in the blood interrupt "remodeling"—an ongoing process in which old, damaged pieces of bone are replaced with new ones.

Inflammation of the gastrointestinal tract (as with inflammatory bowel disease) can be especially detrimental to bone health, because it can prevent absorption of important bone-building nutrients such as calcium and vitamin D. Another inflammatory disease, rheumatoid arthritis, can also have implications because it limits people's physical activity and can keep them from performing weight-bearing, bone-strengthening exercises.

12. It Affects Your Skin

The effects of inflammation aren't just internal: They can also be reflected on your skin. Psoriasis, for example, is an inflammatory condition that occurs when the immune system causes skin cells to grow too quickly. A 2013 study published in JAMA Dermatology suggested that losing weight could help psoriasis patients find relief, since obesity contributes to inflammation.

Chronic inflammation has also been shown to contribute to faster cell aging in animal studies, and some experts believe it also plays a role (along with UV exposure and other environmental effects) in the formation of wrinkles and visible signs of aging.

13. It's Linked With Depression

Inflammation in the brain may be linked to depression, according to a 2015 study published in JAMA Psychiatry; specifically, it may be responsible for depressive symptoms such as low mood, lack of appetite, and poor sleep. Previous research has found that people with depression have higher levels of inflammation in their blood, as well.

"Depression is a complex illness and we know that it takes more than one biological change to tip someone into an episode," said Jeffrey Meyer, MD, senior author of the 2015 study, in a press release. "But we now believe that inflammation in the brain is one of these changes and that's an important step forward." Treating depression with anti-inflammatory medication may be one area of future research, he added.

What is the anti-inflammatory diet?

The anti-inflammatory diet is an eating plan designed to reduce or prevent inflammation. Much like a plant-based diet, the anti-inflammatory diet is a style of eating that encompasses many different types of diets, including the Mediterranean diet, the DASH diet, and the vegetarian diet.

In theory following an anti-inflammatory diet is straightforward. You simply need to consume more anti-inflammatory foods – fruits and vegetables, whole grains, plant-based proteins (like beans and nuts), healthy fats, herbs and spices, and foods rich in omega-3 fatty acids – and reduce your intake of inflammatory foods, such as added sugars, refined carbs and other highly-processed foods, red meats and alcohol.

Fruit and vegetables are good sources of antioxidants, which have a natural anti-inflammatory action.

Antioxidants and omega-3 fatty acids possess anti-inflammatory properties. The antioxidants found abundantly in the fresh produce aisle of the supermarket protect your cells from the effects of free radicals – unstable atoms that damage cells, protein and DNA in a process called oxidative stress, causing illness and ageing.

'Fruit and vegetables are good sources of antioxidants such as polyphenols, which have a natural anti-inflammatory action,' says Dr Brewer. 'Used by plants to protect against ultraviolet radiation and attack by viruses, fungi and bacteria, they provide beneficial anti-inflammatory actions for us too, and help to damp down inflammation.'

Omega-3 fatty acids are found abundantly in fish and other seafood, as well as nuts and seeds, such as flaxseed, chia seeds and walnuts. They reduce the production of molecules released during your body's inflammatory response, such as cytokines. Omega-3 supplements have also shown beneficial anti-inflammatory effects in clinical trials, The Norwegian University of Science and Technology found.

Anti-inflammatory foods

An anti-inflammatory diet should provide a balance of protein, carbs, and fat at every meal, along with vitamins, minerals and fibre. Foods that may help manage or reduce inflammation include:

Fruits and vegetables

All fruits and vegetables fight inflammation in some way. Fill up on cruciferous vegetables, such as broccoli, cauliflower, Brussels sprouts and kale – they contain sulforaphane, which fights inflammation by reducing your levels of cytokines. Berries such as strawberries, blueberries, raspberries and blackberries contain potent antioxidants known as anthocyanins. Citrus fruits, tomatoes, mushrooms, peppers and grapes are also well-documented as potent inflammation-fighting produce.

Aim to eat five to nine servings of fruits and vegetables each day.

Whole grains

Unlike their refined counterparts, whole grains like oats, brown rice and whole wheat bread are high in fibre, antioxidant-rich and nutrient-dense. In a meta-analysis published in the journal Medicine, diets rich in whole grains were associated with a significant decrease in inflammatory markers such as CRP – and as such, helped to reduce systemic inflammation.

Swap refined grains for foods that list a whole grain as the first ingredient.

Pulses

Pulses include all beans, peas and lentils. They are high in fibre, antioxidants, and magnesium, which is known for its inflammation-dampening properties (incidentally, low magnesium intake is linked to incidence of chronic inflammation). Incorporate back beans, chickpeas, garden peas, lentils, kidney beans, runner beans into your recipes.

Replace the red meat usually found in dishes like chilli and bolognese with beans, peas and lentils.

Healthy fats

There are two kinds of healthy fats: Monounsaturated fats, found in nuts, seeds and avocados, and polyunsaturated fats, found in fish and certain nuts and seeds. Both are packed with inflammation-fighting antioxidants. Olive oil is especially potent – it contains oleocanthal, which has been shown to work similarly to ibuprofen. And the anti-inflammatory properties of avocados are so powerful, they've been shown to offset less-healthy foods.

Swap out butter, margarine and vegetable oils for olive oil, avocados, and nuts and seeds.

Fatty fish

The omega-3 fatty acids found in oily fish have been shown to prevent the formation of inflammatory compounds and also help destroy them. The likes of sardines, salmon and rainbow trout are packed with EPA and DHA – these fatty acids are metabolised into resolvins and protectins, which have proven anti-inflammatory effects. These omega-3s can be found in pine nuts, walnuts, flax and sunflower seeds but are less accessible.

Eat more foods rich in omega-3 fatty acids, such as flaxseed, walnuts and oily fish.

Herbs and spices

Herbs and spices are rich in vitamins, minerals, phytonutrients and compounds that act as potent anti-inflammatory agents. Turmeric contains curcumin, chilli peppers contain capsaicin, black pepper contains piperine, and rosemary contains rosmarinic acid and carnosic acid – all of which have been proven to fight inflammation.

Rather than seasoning your meals with salt, experiment with other flavour-enhancers like garlic and ginger.

Coffee, tea and dark chocolate

Coffee, tea (especially green tea) and dark chocolate are rich in phytonutrients, such as polyphenols, which help to tackle inflammation. They also contain caffeine, which offers protection against inflammation in the brain.

Be sure to choose dark chocolate that contains at least 70 per cent cocoa or higher to reap the anti-inflammatory benefits, and enjoy your tea or coffee without added sugar or syrups, which release pro-inflammatory substances in the body.

Inflammatory foods to avoid

Certain foods and drinks can make chronic inflammation worse. When following an anti-inflammatory diet, try to avoid (or limit your intake) of the following foods:

- Processed foods, such as crisps and crackers
- Processed meats, such as hot dogs and sausages
- Foods with added sugar or salt
- Refined carbs, such as white bread, white pasta and baked goods
- Excessive alcohol consumption
- Sugar-sweetened drinks and fruit juice
- Desserts, such as ice cream, biscuits and cakes
- Processed seed and vegetable oils, like sunflower and peanut oil
- Dairy products, such as milk, cheese, butter, and margarine

Some people find they experience an inflammatory reaction when they eat gluten, while others report issues with plants belonging to the nightshade family, such as tomatoes, aubergine and peppers. If you experience this, speak to your doctor. They may recommend omitting these foods from your diet for two weeks to see if the symptoms improve.

Why diet may be more important than weight

Anti-inflammatory diet sample menu

What might an anti-inflammatory diet look like over the course of a day? Below, Dr Brewer shares her recommendations for 24 hours of anti-inflammatory eating:

- Breakfast: Smoked salmon with omega-3-enriched scrambled eggs and fresh fruit juice.

- Lunch: A large mixed salad with watercress, spinach leaves, rocket, fresh herbs, avocado, pecan nuts, pomegranate, humus, mixed beans, coleslaw, and a dressing made with walnut oil, lemon juice and black garlic.

- Dinner: Mackerel with roasted Mediterranean vegetables – aubergines, peppers, tomatoes, red onions, courgettes – and sweet potatoes.

- Snack and drink: Fresh fruit, plus water and herbal tea.

How to support an anti-inflammatory diet

To support your anti-inflammatory diet beyond your weekly shop, incorporate these lifestyle tips or consider taking a specialist supplement:

Lose weight

One of the most successful ways of reducing inflammation in the body is to lose any excess weight. 'This is especially beneficial if you tend to store fat around your waist,' says Dr Brewer. 'Losing weight reduces the production of inflammatory chemicals from fat cells.'

Exercise

Light exercise options, such as walking and cycling, are most beneficial to chronic inflammation. 'Over-exercising can make inflammation worse, due to the production of free radicals in exercising muscle,' Dr Brewer says.

Get enough rest

Losing sleep for even part of one night can trigger the key cellular pathway that produces inflammation, according to research published in the journal Elsevier. So be sure to prioritise your 40 winks.

Take glucosamine

Glucosamine supplements have a powerful anti-inflammatory action, says Dr Brewer. 'It's as effective in treating severe osteoarthritic knee pain as the prescribed anti-inflammatory drug, celecoxib,' she says. 'Its anti-inflammatory action has also been associated with longevity due to reduced risks of heart disease and stroke.'

Try Devil's Claw

Devil's Claw is a traditional herbal remedy that contains anti-inflammatory substances like harpagoside, Dr Brewer continues. 'It can significantly improve inflammation-related rheumatic pain and stiffness in muscles and joints, including back pain.'

Turmeric supplements may help

Turmeric contains curcumin, 'a powerful anti-inflammatory antioxidant that helps to reduce pain and swelling,' says Dr Brewer. 'It does this in a number of ways, including blocking the effects of TNF-alpha (tumour necrosis factor-alpha) which is

implicated in many serious inflammatory diseases.'
So curcumin supplements may also be beneficial.

Experiment with CBD

You could also try CBD (cannabidiol) oil. CBD has analgesic and anti-inflammatory properties, Dr Brewer adds. 'It interacts with our own endocannabinoid receptors to help regulate inflammation,' she says. 'Evolving science suggests that CBD can help to reverse chronic inflammation by blocking TNF-alpha in a complementary way to turmeric.'

Why You'll Love The Anti-Inflammatory Diet

Need some more convincing? Here are just a few reasons why the anti-inflammatory diet might be worth trying.

You don't need to cut carbs.

If you consider yourself the Carbs Queen, you can breathe a sigh of relief. While an anti-inflammatory diet will involve cutting down on processed grains (think: white bread, pasta), you can still enjoy plenty of whole grains (like quinoa or oats) as well as sweet potatoes to get your carb fix.

You can still eat snacks.

If your body is telling you to eat, an anti-inflammatory diet won't stop you. Just focus on snacks like nuts or fruit (an apple with peanut butter is a solid option) as opposed to a sugar-packed granola bar.

You can still pack your foods with flavor.

No bland shakes or meal replacement bars on this plan. Instead, you'll be focusing on filling your plate with colorful foods and ramping up the flavor with spices like cinnamon, ginger, cayenne, and turmeric.

How to Follow this Meal Plan for 30 Days:

To make this plan more manageable, we break it down week-by-week and include meal-prep tips at the start of each week that we encourage you to follow as it makes each day a bit easier. However, don't be afraid to make swaps. If a recipe calls for peanut butter but you have almond butter in the pantry, feel free to make that swap. The same goes for milk use your milk of choice.

Feel free to change around the meals for on specific days based on what you prefer or have in the house. We choose an array of meal options to show some different choices that fit within the anti-inflammatory diet, but if you're someone who finds it easier to have the same breakfast for an entire week, then feel free! In our meal plans, we aim to have a similar calorie range for each meal which means that you can swap recipes for each meal without changing the calorie levels drastically.

And last but not least, don't feel like you have to follow this meal plan or a full 30 days in order to get the anti-inflammatory effects. Use it as healthy eating inspiration and do what feels good to you whether it's one meal or one week!

Week 1

How to Meal-Prep Your Week of Meals:

- Prepare Chopped Veggie Grain Bowls with Turmeric Dressing to have for lunch on Days 2 through 5.

Day 1

Breakfast (310 calories)
- 1 serving Raspberry-Kefir Power Smoothie
- 1 medium orange
- A.M. Snack (206 calories)
- 1/4 cup dry-roasted unsalted almonds

Lunch (360 calories)

- 1 serving White Bean & Veggie Salad
- P.M. Snack (194 calories)
- 1 plum
- 1/4 cup dried walnut halves

Dinner (422 calories)

- 1 serving Greek Roasted Fish with Vegetables

Daily Totals: 1,493 calories, 64 g protein, 135 g carbohydrates, 37 g fiber, 85 g fat, 989 mg sodium

To Make it 1,200 Calories: Change the A.M. snack to 1 clementine and reduce the walnuts at the P.M. snack to 5 dried walnut halves.

To Make it 2,000 Calories: Add 1 whole-wheat English muffin with 2 Tbsp. natural peanut butter to breakfast and add 1 serving Everything Bagel Avocado Toast to lunch.

Day 2

Breakfast (310 calories)
- 1 serving Raspberry-Kefir Power Smoothie
- 1 medium orange
- A.M. Snack (164 calories)
- 1/4 cup dried walnut halves

Lunch (437 calories)
- 1 serving Chopped Veggie Grain Bowls with Turmeric Dressing
- 1 large pear
- P.M. Snack (95 calories)
- 1 medium apple

Dinner (519 calories)

- 1 serving Mediterranean Chicken Quinoa Bowl

Daily Totals: 1,524 calories, 60 g protein, 199 g carbohydrates, 39 g fiber, 59 g fat, 910 mg sodium

To Make it 1,200 Calories: Omit the orange at breakfast and change both the A.M. and P.M. snack to 1/4 cup sliced cucumbers.

To Make it 2,000 Calories: Add 1 large pear and increase to 1/3 cup dried walnuts at A.M. snack and add 3 Tbsp. natural peanut butter to P.M. snack.

Day 3

Breakfast (361 calories)

- 1 serving Egg Salad Avocado Toast

- 1 large pear
- A.M. Snack (140 calories)
- 3/4 cup low-fat plain Greek yogurt
- 1/4 cup raspberries

Lunch (400 calories)

- 1 serving Chopped Veggie Grain Bowls with Turmeric Dressing
- 1 medium apple
- P.M. Snack (164 calories)
- 1/4 cup dried walnuts

Dinner (428 calories)

- 1 serving Kale & Avocado Salad with Blueberries & Edamame
- 1-oz. slice whole-wheat baguette

Daily Totals: 1,493 calories, 58 g protein, 172 g carbohydrates, 39 g fiber, 71 g fat, 1,410 mg sodium

To Make it 1,200 Calories: Omit the pear at breakfast and the raspberries at the A.M. snack plus change the P.M. snack to 1/4 cup sliced cucumbers.

To Make it 2,000 Calories: Add 3 Tbsp. slivered almonds to A.M. snack, add 1 large pear and increase to 20 dried walnut halves at P.M. snack plus add 1 serving Everything Bagel Avocado Toast to dinner.

Day 4

Breakfast (361 calories)
- 1 serving Egg Salad Avocado Toast
- 1 large pear
- A.M. Snack (30 calories)
- 1 plum

Lunch (400 calories)

- 1 serving Chopped Veggie Grain Bowls with Turmeric Dressing
- 1 medium apple
- P.M. Snack (164 calories)
- 1/4 cup dried walnut halves

Dinner (523 calories)

- 1 serving Skillet Lemon Chicken & Potatoes with Kale
- 2 cups mixed greens
- 1 serving Citrus Vinaigrette

Daily Totals: 1.479 calories, 54 g protein, 166 g carbohydrates, 35 g fiber, 72 g fat, 1,126 mg sodium

To Make it 1,200 Calories: Omit the pear at breakfast and omit the mixed greens with Citrus Vinaigrette at dinner.

To Make it 2,000 Calories: Add 25 dry-roasted unsalted almonds to A.M. snack and add 1 avocado, sliced, to dinner.

Day 5

Breakfast (361 calories)
- 1 serving Egg Salad Avocado Toast
- 1 large pear
- A.M. Snack (140 calories)
- 3/4 cup low-fat plain Greek yogurt
- 1/4 cup blackberries

Lunch (400 calories)
- 1 serving Chopped Veggie Grain Bowls with Turmeric Dressing
- 1 medium apple
- P.M. Snack (164 calories)
- 1/4 cup dried walnut halves

Dinner (415 calories)

- 1 serving Spinach Salad with Roasted Sweet Potatoes, White Beans & Basil

Daily Totals: 1,480 calories, 57 g protein, 183 g carbohydrate, 45 g fiber, 65 g fat, 1,181 mg sodium

To Make it 1,200 Calories: Omit the pear at breakfast and the blackberries at the A.M. snack and change the P.M. snack to 1 clementine.

To Make it 2,000 Calories: Add 3 Tbsp. slivered almonds to A.M. snack, add 1 large pear plus increase to 20 dried walnut halves at P.M. snack and add 1 serving Everything Bagel Avocado Toast to dinner.

Day 6

Breakfast (310 calories)

- 1 serving Raspberry-Kefir Power Smoothie
- 1 medium orange
- A.M. Snack (140 calories)
- 3/4 cup low-fat plain Greek yogurt
- 1/4 cup raspberries

Lunch (417 calories)

- 1 serving Salmon-Salad Stuffed Avocado
- 1 medium apple
- P.M. Snack (139 calories)
- 18 dry-roasted unsalted almonds

Dinner (471 calories)

- 1 serving Vegan Coconut Chickpea Curry

Daily Totals: 1,477 calories, 65 g protein, 174 g carbohydrates, 38 g fiber, 63 g fat, 1,159 mg sodium

To Make it 1,200 Calories: Omit the orange at breakfast, reduce the yogurt to 1/2 cup and omit the raspberries at the A.M. snack plus change the P.M. snack to 1/4 cup sliced cucumbers.

To Make it 2,000 Calories: Add 1 slice whole wheat toast with 1 Tbsp. natural peanut butter to breakfast, add 3 Tbsp. slivered almonds to A.M. snack plus add 1 medium apple and increase to 30 almonds at the P.M. snack.

Day 7

Breakfast (310 calories)

- 1 serving Raspberry-Kefir Power Smoothie
- 1 medium orange
- A.M. Snack (206 calories)
- 1/4 cup dry-roasted unsalted almonds

Lunch (417 calories)

- 1 serving Salmon-Salad Stuffed Avocado
- 1 medium apple
- P.M. Snack (130 calories)
- 1 large pear

Dinner (429 calories)

- 1 serving Charred Shrimp & Pesto Buddha Bowls

Daily Totals: 1,494 calories, 71 g protein, 164 g carbohydrates, 41 g fiber, 70 g fat, 1,098 mg sodium

To Make it 1,200 Calories: Omit the orange at breakfast, change the A.M. snack to 1 plum and change the P.M. snack to 1 medium apple.

To Make it 2,000 Calories: Add 1 whole-wheat English muffin with 2 Tbsp. natural peanut butter to breakfast and add 1/4 cup dried walnut halves to P.M. snack.

Week 2

Make three servings Blueberry Almond Chia Pudding to have for breakfast on Days 9 through 11. Prepare Sweet Potato, Kale & Chicken Salad with Peanut Dressing to have for lunch on Days 9 through

12.

Day 8

Breakfast (296 calories)
- 1 serving Spinach & Egg Scramble with Raspberries
- A.M. Snack (305 calories)
- 1 medium apple

- 2 Tbsp. natural peanut butter

Lunch (325 calories)
- 1 serving Green Salad with Edamame & Beets
- P.M. Snack (131 calories)
- 1 large pear

Dinner (447 calories)
- 1 serving Roasted Salmon with Smoky Chickpeas & Greens

Daily Totals: 1,503 calories, 82 g protein, 136 g carbohydrates, 38 g fiber, 70 g fat, 1,742 mg sodium

To Make it 1,200 Calories: Omit the peanut butter at A.M. snack and change the P.M. snack to 1 plum.

To Make it 2,000 Calories: Add 1 serving Everything Bagel Avocado Toast and 1 plum to lunch and add 1/3 cup dry-roasted unsalted almonds to P.M. snack.

Day 9

Breakfast (360 calories)
- 1 serving Blueberry Almond Chia Pudding
- 10 dried walnut halves
- A.M. Snack (95 calories)
- 1 medium apple

Lunch (393 calories)
- 1 serving Sweet Potato, Kale & Chicken Salad with Peanut Dressing
- P.M. Snack (206 calories)
- 1/4 cup dry-roasted unsalted almonds

Dinner (434 calories)

- 1 serving Basil Pesto Pasta with Grilled Vegetables

Daily Totals: 1,488 calories, 58 g protein, 134 g carbohydrates, 33 g fiber, 87 g fat, 1,072 mg sodium

To Make it 1,200 Calories: Omit the walnuts at breakfast and change the P.M. snack to 1 plum.

To Make it 2,000 Calories: Add 3 Tbsp. natural peanut butter to A.M. snack, add 1 medium orange to lunch and add 1 large pear to P.M. snack.

Day 10

Breakfast (360 calories)

- 1 serving Blueberry Almond Chia Pudding
- 10 dried walnut halves

- A.M. Snack (140 calories)
- 3/4 cup low-fat plain Greek yogurt
- 1/4 cup raspberries

Lunch (393 calories)

- 1 serving Sweet Potato, Kale & Chicken Salad with Peanut Dressing
- P.M. Snack (131 calories)
- 1 large pear

Dinner (492 calories)

- 1 serving Celeriac & Walnut Tacos
- 1 serving Jason Mraz's Guacamole

Daily Totals: 1,515 calories, 65 g protein, 155 g carbohydrates, 41 g fiber, 78 g fat, 1,198 mg sodium

To Make it 1,200 Calories: Omit the walnuts at breakfast and omit the raspberries at the A.M.

snack plus reduce the yogurt to 1/2 cup and change the P.M. snack to 1/4 cup sliced cucumbers.

To Make it 2,000 Calories: Add 3 Tbsp. chopped walnuts to A.M. snack, add 1 medium orange to lunch and add 1/3 cup dry-roasted unsalted almonds to P.M. snack.

Day 11

Breakfast (360 calories)

- 1 serving Blueberry Almond Chia Pudding
- 10 dried walnut halves
- A.M. Snack (131 calories)
- 1 large pear

Lunch (393 calories)

- 1 serving Sweet Potato, Kale & Chicken Salad with Peanut Dressing

- P.M. Snack (206 calories)
- 1/4 cup almonds

Dinner (402 calories)
- 1 serving Mediterranean Chicken with Orzo Salad

Daily Totals: 1,492 calories, 79 g protein, 136 g carbohydrates, 35 g fiber, 75 g fat, 1,173 mg sodium

To Make it 1,200 Calories: Change the A.M. snack to 1 plum and the P.M. snack to 1 clementine.

To Make it 2,000 Calories: Add 1/3 cup dried walnut halves to A.M. snack, 1 medium apple to P.M. snack and add 1 serving Everything Bagel Avocado Toast to dinner.

Day 12

Breakfast (290 calories)

- 1 serving Sprouted-Grain Toast with Peanut Butter & Banana
- A.M. Snack (131 calories)
- 1 large pear

Lunch (393 calories)

- 1 serving Sweet Potato, Kale & Chicken Salad with Peanut Dressing
- P.M. Snack (225 calories)
- 1 medium apple
- 10 dried walnut halves

Dinner (466 calories)

- 1 serving Quinoa Power Salad

Daily Totals: 1,505 calories, 72 g protein, 175 g carbohydrates, 31 g fiber, 59 g fat, 1,416 mg sodium

To Make it 1,200 Calories: Change the A.M. snack to 1 plum and the P.M. snack to 1 clementine.

To Make it 2,000 Calories: Increase to 2 servings Sprouted-Grain Toast with Peanut Butter & Banana at breakfast and add 1/4 cup dry-roasted unsalted almonds to A.M. snack.

Day 13

Breakfast (290 calories)
- 1 serving Sprouted-Grain Toast with Peanut Butter & Banana
- A.M. Snack (166 calories)
- 1 cup low-fat plain Greek yogurt

Lunch (360 calories)

- 1 serving White Bean & Veggie Salad
- P.M. Snack (206 calories)
- 1/4 cup dry-roasted unsalted almonds

Dinner (481 calories)

- 1 serving Quinoa, Chicken & Broccoli Salad with Roasted Lemon Dressing

Daily Totals: 1,503 calories, 70 g protein, 134 g carbohydrates, 32 g fiber, 83 g fat, 894 mg sodium

To Make it 1,200 Calories: Change the A.M. snack to 1 medium orange and the P.M. snack to 1 plum.

To Make it 2,000 Calories: Increase to 2 servings Sprouted-Grain Toast with Peanut Butter & Banana at breakfast and add 1/4 cup dried walnut halves to A.M. snack.

Day 14

Breakfast (296 calories)

- 1 serving Spinach & Egg Scramble with Raspberries
- A.M. Snack (186 calories)
- 1 cup low-fat plain Greek yogurt
- 1/3 cup blueberries

Lunch (360 calories)

- 1 serving White Bean & Veggie Salad
- P.M. Snack (216 calories)
- 1/3 cup dried walnut halves

Dinner (421 calories)

- 1 serving Spicy Shrimp Tacos

Daily Totals: 1,478 calories, 76 g protein, 105 g carbohydrates, 32 g fiber, 90 g fat, 1,677 mg sodium

To Make it 1,200 Calories: Omit the yogurt at the A.M. snack and reduce the walnuts to 10 dried walnut halves.

To Make it 2,000 Calories: Add 1/3 cup dry-roasted unsalted almonds to A.M. snack and add 1 serving Guacamole Chopped Salad to dinner.

Week 3

Prepare Brussels Sprouts Salad with Crunchy Chickpeas to have for lunch on Days 16 through 29.

Make Cinnamon Roll Overnight Oats to have for breakfast on Days 16 through 20.

Day 15

Breakfast (290 calories)

- 1 serving Sprouted-Grain Toast with Peanut Butter & Banana
- A.M. Snack (131 calories)
- 1 large pear

Lunch (387 calories)

- 1 serving Green Salad with Edamame & Beets
- 1 medium orange
- P.M. Snack (206 calories)
- 1/4 cup dry-roasted unsalted almonds

Dinner (473 calories)

- 1 serving Walnut-Rosemary Crusted Salmon
- 1 serving Panzanella with Tomatoes & Grilled Corn

Daily Totals: 1,488 calories, 66 g protein, 157 g carbohydrates, 35 g fiber, 71 g fat, 1,370 mg sodium

To Make it 1,200 Calories: Change the A.M. snack to 1 plum and the P.M. snack to 1 clementine.

To Make it 2,000 Calories: Increase to 2 servings Sprouted-Grain Toast with Peanut Butter & Banana and add 1/3 cup dried walnut halves to A.M. snack.

Day 16

Breakfast (291 calories)

- 1 serving Cinnamon Roll Overnight Oats
- 1 medium apple
- A.M. Snack (164 calories)
- 1/4 cup dried walnut halves

Lunch (337 calories)

- 1 serving Brussels Sprouts Salad with Crunchy Chickpeas
- P.M. Snack (187 calories)

- 1 cup low-fat plain Greek yogurt
- 1/4 cup blueberries

Dinner (498 calories)
- 1 serving Chicken, Quinoa & Sweet Potato Casserole
- 2 cups mixed greens
- 1 serving Citrus Vinaigrette

Meal-Prep Tip: reserve leftover Chicken, Quinoa & Sweet Potato Casserole to have for dinner tomorrow

Daily Totals: 1,476 calories, 69 g protein, 151 g carbohydrates, 32 g fiber, 70 g fat, 1,385 mg sodium

To Make it 1,200 Calories: Change the A.M. snack to 1 plum and omit the yogurt at the P.M. snack.

To Make it 2,000 Calories: Add 1 serving Raspberry-Kefir Power Smoothie to breakfast, add 3 Tbsp. slivered almonds to P.M. snack and add 1/2 an avocado, sliced, to dinner.

Day 17

Breakfast (291 calories)
- 1 serving Cinnamon Roll Overnight Oats
- 1 medium apple
- A.M. Snack (187 calories)
- 1 cup low-fat plain Greek yogurt
- 1/4 cup blueberries

Lunch (337 calories)
- 1 serving Brussels Sprouts Salad with Crunchy Chickpeas
- P.M. Snack (206 calories)
- 1/4 cup dry-roasted unsalted almonds

Dinner (498 calories)

- 1 serving Chicken, Quinoa & Sweet Potato Casserole
- 2 cups mixed greens
- 1 serving Citrus Vinaigrette

Daily Totals: 1,519 calories, 73 g protein, 155 g carbohydrates, 35 g fiber, 72 g fat, 1,385 mg sodium

To Make it 1,200 Calories: Omit the yogurt at the A.M. snack and change the P.M. snack to 1 plum.

To Make it 2,000 Calories: Add 1 serving Raspberry-Kefir Power Smoothie to breakfast, add 2 Tbsp. slivered almonds to P.M. snack and add 1/2 an avocado, sliced, to dinner.

Day 18

Breakfast (291 calories)

- 1 serving Cinnamon Roll Overnight Oats
- 1 medium apple
- A.M. Snack (131 calories)
- 1 large pear

Lunch (337 calories)

- 1 serving Brussels Sprouts Salad with Crunchy Chickpeas
- P.M. Snack (164 calories)
- 1/4 cup dried walnut halves

Dinner (599 calories)

- 1 serving Chicken Massaman Curry with Turmeric Brown Rice

Daily Totals: 1,521 calories, 52 g protein, 208 g carbohydrates, 38 g fiber, 61 g fat, 1,483 mg sodium

To Make it 1,200 Calories: Omit the apple at breakfast, change the A.M. snack to 1 plum and change the P.M. snack to 1 clementine.

To Make it 2,000 Calories: Add 1/3 cup dry-roasted unsalted almonds to A.M. snack, 1 medium orange to lunch and 1 large pear to P.M. snack.

Day 19

Breakfast (291 calories)

- 1 serving Cinnamon Roll Overnight Oats
- 1 medium apple
- A.M. Snack (305 calories)
- 1 medium apple
- 2 Tbsp. natural peanut butter

Lunch (337 calories)

- 1 serving Brussels Sprouts Salad with Crunchy Chickpeas
- P.M. Snack (164 calories)
- 1/4 cup dried walnut halves

Dinner (402 calories)

- 1 serving Mediterranean Cod with Roasted Tomatoes
- 1 serving Guacamole Chopped Salad

Daily Totals: 1,498 calories, 54 g protein, 145 g carbohydrates, 41 g fiber, 84 g fat, 1,407 mg sodium

To Make it 1,200 Calories: Omit the peanut butter at the A.M. snack and change the P.M. snack to 1 medium orange.

To Make it 2,000 Calories: Add 1 serving Raspberry-Kefir Power Smoothie, 1 large apple to lunch and 1 large pear to P.M. snack.

Day 20

Breakfast (291 calories)

- 1 serving Cinnamon Roll Overnight Oats
- 1 medium apple
- A.M. Snack (228 calories)
- 1 1/4 cup low-fat plain Greek yogurt
- 1/4 cup blueberries

Lunch (351 calories)

- 1 serving Avocado Egg Salad Sandwiches
- P.M. Snack (131 calories)
- 1 large pear

Dinner (504 calories)

- 1 serving Greek Salad with Edamame
- 1/2 avocado, sliced

Daily Totals: 1,505 calories, 71 g protein, 170 g carbohydrates, 40 g fiber, 67 g fat, 1,554 mg sodium

To Make it 1,200 Calories: Omit the yogurt at the A.M. snack and change the P.M. snack to 1 clementine.

To Make it 2,000 Calories: Add 1 serving Raspberry-Kefir Power Smoothie to breakfast, 1 clementine to lunch and 1/3 cup dried walnut halves to P.M. snack.

Day 21

Breakfast (290 calories)

- 1 serving Sprouted-Grain Toast with Peanut Butter & Banana
- A.M. Snack (262 calories)
- 1 large pear
- 10 dried walnut halves

Lunch (351 calories)

- 1 serving Avocado Egg Salad Sandwiches
- P.M. Snack (95 calories)
- 1 medium apple

Dinner (482)

- 1 serving Honey Walnut Shrimp
- 1/2 cup cooked brown rice

Daily Totals: 1,479 calories, 58 g protein, 178 g carbohydrates, 30 g fiber, 66 g fat, 972 mg sodium

To Make it 1,200 Calories: Change the A.M. snack to 1 plum and change the P.M. to 1 medium orange.

To Make it 2,000 Calories: Increase to 2 servings Sprouted-Grain Toast with Peanut Butter & Banana at breakfast and add 2 Tbsp. natural peanut butter to P.M. snack.

Week 4

Make 3 servings Blueberry Almond Chia Pudding to have for breakfast on Days 23 through 25.

Prepare Vegan Superfood Buddha Bowls to have for lunch on Days 23 through 26.

Day 22

Breakfast (296 calories)

- 1 serving Spinach & Egg Scramble with Raspberries
- A.M. Snack (182 calories)
- 1 cup low-fat plain Greek yogurt
- 1/4 cup raspberries

Lunch (387 calories)

- 1 serving Green Salad with Edamame & Beets
- 1 medium orange
- P.M. Snack (139 calories)
- 18 dry-roasted unsalted almonds

Dinner (480 calories)

- 1 serving Mushroom Shawarma with Yogurt-Tahini Sauce
- 1 serving Cucumber & Avocado Salad

Daily Totals: 1,483 calories, 78 g protein, 118 g carbohydrates, 35 g fiber, 82 g fat, 1,993 mg sodium

To Make it 1,200 Calories: Omit the yogurt at the A.M. snack and change the P.M. snack to 1/4 cup blueberries.

To Make it 2,000 Calories: Add 1 serving Raspberry-Kefir Power Smoothie to breakfast and increase to 1/3 cup almonds plus add 1 large pear to P.M. snack.

Day 23

Breakfast (339 calories)
- 1 serving Blueberry Almond Chia Pudding
- 1 cup low-fat plain kefir
- A.M. Snack (260 calories)
- 1 cup low-fat plain Greek yogurt
- 1/4 cup raspberries
- 2 Tbsp. slivered almonds

Lunch (381 calories)
- 1 serving Vegan Superfood Buddha Bowls

- P.M. Snack (95 calories)
- 1 medium apple

Dinner (434 calories)

- 1 serving Basil Pesto Pasta with Grilled Vegetables
- Daily Totals: 1,508 calories, 70 g protein, 163 g carbohydrates, 39 g fiber, 72 g fat, 822 mg sodium

- To Make it 1,200 Calories: Omit the yogurt and slivered almonds at the A.M. snack and change the P.M. snack to 1/4 cup blueberries.

To Make it 2,000 Calories: Add 1 serving Sprouted-Grain Toast with Peanut Butter & Banana to breakfast and add 2 Tbsp. natural peanut butter to P.M. snack.

.

Day 24

Breakfast (339 calories)

- 1 serving Blueberry Almond Chia Pudding
- 1 cup low-fat plain kefir
- A.M. Snack (62 calories)
- 1 medium orange

Lunch (381 calories)

- 1 serving Vegan Superfood Buddha Bowls
- P.M. Snack (206 calories)
- 1/4 cup dry-roasted unsalted almonds

Dinner (519 calories)

- 1 serving Mediterranean Chicken Quinoa Bowl

Daily Totals: 1,506 calories, 75 g protein, 139 g carbohydrates, 34 g fiber, 77 g fat, 1,071 mg sodium

To Make it 1,200 Calories: Omit the kefir at breakfast and change the P.M. snack to 1/4 cup blueberries.

To Make it 2,000 Calories: Add 1 serving Sprouted-Grain Toast with Peanut Butter & Banana to breakfast and add 16 dried walnut halves to A.M. snack.

Day 25

Breakfast (339 calories)
- 1 serving Blueberry Almond Chia Pudding
- 1 cup low-fat plain kefir
- A.M. Snack (95 calories)
- 1 medium apple

Lunch (381 calories)

- 1 serving Vegan Superfood Buddha Bowls
- P.M. Snack (131 calories)
- 1 large pear

Dinner (555 Calories)

- 1 serving Ginger-Tahini Oven-Baked Salmon & Vegetables

Daily Totals: 1,500 calories, 71 g protein, 183 g carbohydrates, 43 g fiber, 62 g fat, 1,109 mg sodium
To Make it 1,200 Calories: Omit the kefir at breakfast, change the A.M. snack to 1 plum and change the P.M. snack to 1/4 cup raspberries.

To Make it 2,000 Calories: Add 1 serving Sprouted-Grain Toast with Peanut Butter & Banana to breakfast and add 2 Tbsp. natural peanut butter to A.M. snack.

Day 26

Breakfast (310 calories)

- 1 serving Raspberry-Kefir Power Smoothie
- 1 medium orange
- A.M. Snack (164 calories)
- 1/4 cup dried walnut halves

Lunch (381 calories)

- 1 serving Vegan Superfood Buddha Bowls
- P.M. Snack (131 calories)
- 1 large pear

Dinner (495 calories)

- 1 serving Peanut Zucchini Noodle Salad with Chicken
- 2 cups mixed greens
- 1 serving Citrus Vinaigrette

Daily Totals: 1,481 calories, 58 g protein, 161 g carbohydrates, 40 g fiber, 75 g fat, 1,198 mg sodium

To Make it 1,200 Calories: Omit the orange at breakfast, change the A.M. snack to 1 plum and change the P.M. snack to 1/2 cup blueberries.

To Make it 2,000 Calories: Add 1 serving Sprouted-Grain Toast with Peanut Butter & Banana to breakfast and add 1/4 cup dry-roasted unsalted almonds to P.M. snack.

Day 27

Breakfast (310 calories)
- 1 serving Raspberry-Kefir Power Smoothie
- 1 medium orange
- A.M. Snack (206 calories)
- 1/4 cup dry-roasted unsalted almonds

Lunch (323 calories)

- 1 serving Salmon-Stuffed Avocados
- 1 plum
- P.M. Snack (221 calories)
- 1 cup low-fat plain Greek yogurt
- 1/4 cup raspberries
- 1 Tbsp. slivered almonds

Dinner (429 calories)

- 1 serving Charred Shrimp & Pesto Buddha Bowls

Daily Totals: 1,490 calories, 95 g protein, 125 g carbohydrates, 33 g fiber, 75 g fat, 1,123 mg sodium

To Make it 1,200 Calories: Change the A.M. snack to 1 plum and omit the yogurt and slivered almonds at the P.M. snack.

To Make it 2,000 Calories: Add 1 serving Sprouted-Grain Toast with Peanut Butter & Banana to breakfast plus increase to 1/3 cup almonds and add 1 large pear to A.M. snack.

Day 28

Breakfast (296 calories)

- 1 serving Spinach & Egg Scramble with Raspberries
- A.M. Snack (206 calories)
- 1/4 cup dry-roasted unsalted almonds

Lunch (323 calories)

- 1 serving Salmon-Stuffed Avocados
- 1 plum
- P.M. Snack (236 calories)
- 1 large pear
- 8 dried walnut halves

Dinner (414 calories)

- 1 serving Chicken, Arugula & Butternut Squash Salad with Brussels Sprouts
- 1 serving Everything Bagel Avocado Toast

Meal-Prep Tip: Reserve 2 servings Chicken, Arugula & Butternut Squash Salad with Brussels Sprouts to have for lunch on Days 29 & 30.

Daily Totals: 1,475 calories, 74 g protein, 119 g carbohydrates, 36 g fiber, 86 g fat, 1,427 mg sodium

To Make it 1,200 Calories: Change the A.M. snack to 1 plum and change the P.M. snack to 1 medium orange.

To Make it 2,000 Calories: Add 1 serving Raspberry-Kefir Power Smoothie to breakfast, add 1 medium apple to A.M. snack and increase to 1/3 cup dried walnut halves at P.M. snack.

Week 5

Day 29

Breakfast (310 calories)

- 1 serving Raspberry-Kefir Power Smoothie
- 1 medium orange
- A.M. Snack (206 calories)
- 1/4 cup dry-roasted unsalted almonds

Lunch (373 calories)

- 1 serving Chicken, Arugula & Butternut Squash Salad with Brussels Sprouts
- 1 large pear
- P.M. Snack (221 calories)
- 1 cup low-fat plain Greek yogurt

- 1/4 cup raspberries
- 1 Tbsp. slivered almonds

Dinner (402 calories)
- 1 serving Mediterranean Cod with Roasted Tomatoes
- 1 serving Guacamole Chopped Salad

Daily Totals: 1,512 calories, 84 g protein, 150 g carbohydrates, 39 g fiber, 73 g fat, 1,146 mg sodium

To Make it 1,200 Calories: Change the A.M. snack to 1/4 cup blueberries and change the P.M. snack to 1 medium apple.

To Make it 2,000 Calories: Add 1 serving Sprouted-Grain Toast with Peanut Butter & Banana to breakfast, add 1 large pear to A.M. snack and increase to 3 Tbsp. slivered almonds at P.M. snack.

Day 30

Breakfast (310 calories)

- 1 serving Raspberry-Kefir Power Smoothie
- 1 medium orange
- A.M. Snack (206 calories)
- 1/4 cup dry-roasted unsalted almonds

Lunch (373)

- 1 serving Chicken, Arugula & Butternut Squash Salad with Brussels Sprouts
- 1 large pear
- P.M. Snack (95 calories)
- 1 medium apple

Dinner (504 calories)

- 1 serving Greek Salad with Edamame

- 1/2 avocado, sliced

Daily Totals: 1,488 calories, 54 g protein, 169 g carbohydrates, 45 g fiber, 76 g fat, 949 mg sodium

To Make it 1,200 Calories: Change the A.M. snack to 1 plum and change the P.M. snack to 1/4 cup sliced cucumbers.

To Make it 2,000 Calories: Add 1 serving Sprouted-Grain Toast with Peanut Butter & Banana to breakfast and 2 Tbsp. natural peanut butter to P.M. snack.

Recipes For Anti-inlammatory Diet

Caesar Dressing

Ingredients:

¼ Cup Paleo mayonnaise

2 Tablespoons Olive Oil

2 Cloves Garlic, Minced

½ Teaspoon Anchovy Paste

1 Tablespoon White Wine Vinegar

½ Teaspoon Lemon Zest

2 Tablespoons Lemon Juice, Fresh

Sea Salt & Black Pepper to Taste

Directions:

Whisk all of your ingredients together. It should be emulsified and combined. Put salt and pepper, and then refrigerate it for up to a week.

Beans

Ingredients:

8 Ounces Beans, Dried

Filtered Water (for Soaking & Cooking)

1 Bay leaf

1 Teaspoon Garlic

1 Teaspoon Onion Powder

½ Teaspoon Cumin

Pinch Sea Salt, Fine

Directions:

Get out a glass bowl and add in your beans. Cover them with water, and then add a dash of salt. Soak for eight hours.

Drain them, and make sure to rinse well—transfer to a pot, and then season.

Put about two inches of water, and then cook on high heat. Boil, and then reduce it to low. Allow it to simmer for an hour. Serve.

Lemon Dijon Dressing

Ingredients:

¼ Cup Olive Oil

1 Teaspoon Dijon Mustard

½ Teaspoon Honey, Raw

¼ Teaspoon Basil

1 Clove Garlic, Minced

¼ Teaspoon Sea Salt, Fine

2 Tablespoons Lemon Juice, Fresh

Directions:

Mix all ingredients, and shake vigorously. Refrigerate for up to a week.

Tahini & Lime Dressing

Ingredients:

3 Tablespoons Water

2 Tablespoons Lime Juice Fresh

1 Tablespoon Apple Cider Vinegar

1/3 cup Tahini (Sesame Paste)

1 Teaspoon Lime Zest

1 ½ Teaspoons Honey, Raw

Pinch Sea Salt, Fine

¼ Teaspoon Garlic Powder

Directions:

Combine everything, and shake until combined. Serve.

Everything Aioli

Ingredients:

½ Cup Whole Milk

2 Teaspoons Dijon Mustard

¼ Teaspoon Honey, Raw

½ Teaspoon Hot Sauce

Pinch Sea Salt

Directions:

Mix everything, and it will keep in the fridge for up
to three days.

Almond Romesco Sauce

Ingredients:

2 Red Bell Peppers, Chopped Rough

6 Cherry Tomatoes, Chopped Rough

3 Cloves Garlic, Chopped Rough

½ White Onion, Chopped Rough

1 Tablespoon Avocado Oil

1 cup Raw Almonds, Blanched

¼ Cup Olive Oil

2 Tablespoons Apple Cider Vinegar

Sea Salt & Black Pepper to taste

Directions:

Turn your broiler to high and allow it to preheat.

Get out a baking sheet and line it with foil.

Spread your tomatoes, onion, garlic, and bell pepper onto your baking sheet, and drizzle it with avocado oil. Broil this for ten minutes, and then get out a blender.

Pulse your almonds until they are crumbly.

Add in your olive oil, vinegar, vegetables, salt, and pepper. Process until smooth. It can keep in the fridge for up to five days. Alternatively, you can freeze it, and it will keep for three months.

Honey-Lime Vinaigrette with Fresh Herbs

Ingredients:

Juice of 4 limes

3 tablespoons honey

2 tablespoons apple cider vinegar

2 tablespoons Dijon mustard

2 garlic cloves, minced

3 scallions, finely chopped

½ cup roughly chopped fresh cilantro

Directions:

Whisk the lime juice, honey, vinegar, mustard, and garlic in a medium bowl. Put the scallions and cilantro, stir.

Simple Citrus Vinaigrette Dressing

Ingredients:

Juice of 1 lemon

2 tablespoons apple cider vinegar

2 tablespoons olive oil

½ teaspoon Dijon mustard

1 garlic clove, minced

¾ teaspoon salt

1 teaspoon freshly ground black pepper

½ teaspoon dried oregano

½ teaspoon dried thyme

Directions:

Mixer the lemon juice, vinegar, oil, mustard, garlic, salt, pepper, oregano, and thyme in a medium bowl. Serve.

Zesty Vegan Caesar Dressing

Ingredients:

¼ cup tahini

1 teaspoon Dijon mustard

Juice of 1 lemon

2 teaspoons capers, minced

3 garlic cloves, minced

1 teaspoon maple syrup

½ teaspoon salt

½ teaspoon freshly ground black pepper

1 or 2 tablespoons cold water

Directions:

Mix the tahini, mustard, lemon juice, capers, garlic, maple syrup, salt, and pepper in a medium bowl. Put the water 1 tablespoon at a time if needed to thin the dressing to a pourable consistency.

Creamy Avocado Dressing

Ingredients:

1 avocado, halved and pitted

1 tablespoon olive oil

2 teaspoons apple cider vinegar

1 garlic clove, peeled but whole

Juice of 1 lemon

½ teaspoon onion powder

1 teaspoon maple syrup

1 teaspoon Dijon mustard

½ teaspoon salt

½ teaspoon freshly ground black pepper

10 tablespoons cold water

Directions:

Process the avocado flesh into a food processor. Add the oil, vinegar, garlic, lemon juice, onion powder, maple syrup, mustard, salt, and pepper and pulse the mixture until it's smooth and creamy. Add as much water as you need, 1 tablespoon at a time, to thin it to a thick but pourable consistency.

Simple Ginger Teriyaki Sauce

Ingredients:

¼ cup tamari

3 tablespoons cold water, plus 1½ teaspoons

2 tablespoons honey

2 tablespoons rice vinegar

1 garlic clove, minced

½ teaspoon sriracha

1½ teaspoons grated fresh ginger

1½ teaspoons arrowroot powder or cornstarch

Directions:

Mix the tamari, 3 tablespoons of water, the honey, vinegar, garlic, sriracha, and ginger in a medium bowl. Transfer to a medium saucepan and heat it over medium-high heat.

While the tamari mixture is heating, in a small bowl, combine the remaining 1½ teaspoons of water and the arrowroot powder, mixing well to incorporate. Thicken for at least 2 to 3 minutes.

Once the tamari mixture boils, reduce the heat to medium-low and whisk in the arrowroot mixture.

Continue to whisk the sauce in the pan for 1 to 2 minutes more until it thickens slightly. Set it aside. There will be some larger pieces of garlic and ginger in this sauce. For a smoother sauce, blend in a blender for 10 to 20 seconds, until the ginger and garlic are completely incorporated.

Avocado Crema

Ingredients:

1 avocado, halved and pitted

¼ cup full-fat coconut milk

Juice of 1 lime

¼ teaspoon salt

¼ cup fresh cilantro leaves

Directions:

Process the avocado flesh into a food processor. Add the coconut milk, lime juice, salt, and cilantro and pulse the mixture until it's smooth and creamy.

Basic Brown Rice

Ingredients:

1 cup of brown rice

2½ cups water

½ teaspoon salt

Directions:

Mix the rice, water, plus salt in a medium saucepan.

Simmer, uncovered, over medium-high heat.

Set the heat to low, cover, then simmer within 45

minutes. Do not stir the rice during cooking.

When no liquid remains, remove the pan from the

heat and set it aside to cool for 10 minutes.

Fluff the rice gently using a fork to avoid sticking.

Savory Herbed Quinoa

Ingredients:

1 cup quinoa, rinsed

2 cups vegetable broth

1½ tablespoons olive oil

Juice of ½ lemon

½ teaspoon salt

½ teaspoon freshly ground black pepper

½ cup chopped fresh parsley

½ cup chopped fresh basil

2 scallions, chopped

Directions:

Mix the quinoa and broth in a saucepan and bring to a boil over high heat. Set the heat to medium-low, cover, then simmer for 15 to 20 minutes.

Remove from the heat and let rest, covered, for 10 minutes more.

Transfer to a large bowl and put the olive oil, lemon juice, salt, pepper, parsley, basil, and scallions. Stir to incorporate.

Garlic-Herb Marinated Tempeh or Tofu

Ingredients:

8 ounces tempeh

2 tablespoons olive oil

¼ cup vegetable broth or water

1 tablespoon white wine vinegar

3 garlic cloves, minced

1½ teaspoons dried thyme

½ teaspoon salt

½ teaspoon freshly ground black pepper

Directions:

Preheat the oven to 400°F. Line a sheet pan with parchment paper.

Slice the tempeh in crosswise into 1-inch-thick slices. For the marinade, combine the oil, broth, vinegar, garlic, thyme, salt, and pepper in a large bowl. Place the tempeh in the marinade and use a spoon to coat it thoroughly. Marinate for at least 10 minutes, then flip or toss and marinate for 10 minutes more.

Pour the tempeh onto the sheet pan in a single layer. Pour any additional marinade onto the pan and bake for 15 to 20 minutes.

Turmeric Oven Scrambled Eggs

Ingredients:

8 to 10 large eggs, pasture-raised

½ cup unsweetened almond or coconut milk

½ teaspoon turmeric powder

1 teaspoon chopped cilantro

¼ teaspoon black pepper

A pinch of salt

Directions:

Preheat the oven to 3500F.

Grease a casserole or heat-proof baking dish.

In a bowl, whisk the egg, milk, turmeric powder, black pepper, and salt.

Pour in the egg mixture into the baking dish—Bake within 15 minutes.

Remove, then garnish with chopped cilantro on top.

Breakfast Oatmeal

Ingredients:

2/3 cup coconut milk

1 egg white, pasture-raised

½ cup gluten-free quick-cooking oats

½ teaspoon turmeric powder

½ teaspoon cinnamon

¼ teaspoon ginger

Directions:

Place the non-dairy milk in a saucepan and heat over medium flame.

Stir in the egg white and continue whisking until the mixture becomes smooth.

Put in the rest of the fixing and cook for another 3 minutes.

Blueberry Smoothie

Ingredients:

1 cup almond milk

1 frozen banana

1 cup frozen blueberries

2 handful spinach

1 tablespoon almond butter

¼ teaspoon cinnamon

¼ teaspoon cayenne pepper

1 teaspoon maca powder

Directions:

Pulse all the fixing in a blender until well-combined. Serve immediately.

Breakfast Porridge

Ingredients:

6 tablespoons organic cottage cheese

3 tablespoons flaxseed

3 tablespoons flax oil

2 tablespoons organic raw almond butter

1 tablespoon organic coconut meat

1 tablespoon raw honey

¼ cup of water

Directions:

Combine all ingredients in a bowl. Mix until well combined.

Place in a bowl and chill before serving.

Cherry Spinach Smoothie

Ingredients:

1 cup plain kefir

1 cup frozen cherries, pitted

½ cup baby spinach leaves

¼ cup mashed ripe avocado

1 tablespoon almond butter

1-piece peeled ginger (1/2 inch)

1 teaspoon chia seeds

Directions:

Place all ingredients in a blender. Pulse until smooth.

Allow chilling in the fridge before serving.

Tropical Carrot Ginger and Turmeric Smoothie

Ingredients:

1 blood orange, peeled and seeded

1 large carrot, peeled and chopped

½ cup frozen mango chunks

2/3 cup coconut water

1 tablespoon raw hemp seeds

¾ teaspoon grated ginger

1 ½ teaspoon peeled and grated turmeric

A pinch of cayenne pepper

A pinch of salt

Directions:

Blend all fixings in a blender until smooth.

Chill before serving.

Golden Milk Chia Pudding

Ingredients:

4 cups of coconut milk

3 tablespoons honey

1 teaspoon vanilla extract

1 teaspoon ground turmeric

½ teaspoon ground cinnamon

½ teaspoon ground ginger

¾ cup of coconut yogurt

½ cup chia seeds

1 cup fresh mixed berry

¼ cup toasted coconut chips

Directions:

Mix the coconut milk, honey, vanilla extract, turmeric, cinnamon, and ginger in a bowl. Add in the coconut yogurt.

In bowls, place chia seeds, berries, and coconut chips.

Pour in the milk mixture.

Allow chilling in the fridge to set for 6 hours.

No-Bake Turmeric Protein Donuts

Ingredients:

1 ½ cups raw cashews

½ cup Medjool dates pitted

1 tablespoon vanilla protein powder

½ cup shredded coconut

2 tablespoons maple syrup

¼ teaspoon vanilla extract

1 teaspoon turmeric powder

¼ cup dark chocolate

Directions:

Mix all items except for the chocolate in a food processor.

Pulse until smooth.

Roll batter into 8 balls and press into a silicone donut mold.

Chill for 30 minutes to set.

Meanwhile, make the chocolate topping by melting the chocolate in a double boiler.

Once the donuts have set, remove the donuts from the mold and drizzle with chocolate.

Choco-Nana Pancakes

Ingredients:

2 large bananas, peeled and mashed

2 large eggs, pasture-raised

3 tablespoon cacao powder

2 tablespoons almond butter

1 teaspoon pure vanilla extract

1/8 teaspoon salt

Coconut oil for greasing

Directions:

Preheat a skillet on medium-low heat and grease the pan with coconut oil.

Place all ingredients in a food processor and pulse until smooth.

Pour a batter (about ¼ cup) onto the skillet and form a pancake.

Cook for 3 minutes on each side.

Sweet Potato Cranberry Breakfast bars

Ingredients:

1 ½ cups sweet potato puree

2 tablespoons coconut oil, melted

2 tablespoons maple syrup

2 eggs, pasture-raised

1 cup almond meal

1/3 cup coconut flour

1 ½ teaspoon baking soda

1 cup fresh cranberry, pitted and chopped

¼ cup of water

Directions:

Preheat the oven to 3500F.

Grease a baking pan with coconut oil. Set aside.

Combine the sweet potato puree, water, coconut oil, maple syrup, and eggs in a mixing bowl.

In another bowl, sift the almond flour, coconut flour, and baking soda.

Put the dry fixing to the wet fixing. Mix.

Put into the baking pan and press the cranberries on top.

Bake for 40 minutes or until a toothpick inserted in the middle comes out clean.

Allow to rest or cool before removing from the pan.

Savory Breakfast Pancakes

Ingredients:

½ cup almond flour

½ cup tapioca flour

1 cup of coconut milk

½ teaspoon chili powder

¼ teaspoon turmeric powder

½ red onion, chopped

1 handful cilantro leaves, chopped

½ inch ginger, grated

1 teaspoon salt

¼ teaspoon ground black pepper

Directions:

Mix all the fixing until well-combined in a bowl.

Heat a pan on low, medium heat and grease with oil.

Pour ¼ cup of batter onto the pan and spread the mixture to create a pancake.

Fry for 3 minutes per side.

Scrambled Eggs with Smoked Salmon

Ingredients:

4 eggs

2 tablespoons coconut milk

Fresh chives, chopped

4 slices of wild-caught smoked salmon, chopped

salt to taste

Directions:

Whisk the egg, coconut milk, plus chives in a bowl. Grease the skillet with oil and heat over medium-low heat.

Put the egg batter, then scramble it while cooking. When the eggs start to settle, add in the smoked salmon and cook for 2 more minutes.

Raspberry Grapefruit Smoothie

Ingredients:
Juice from 1 grapefruit, freshly squeezed
1 banana, peeled and sliced
1 cup raspberries

Directions:
Pulse all fixing in a blender until smooth. Chill before serving.

Breakfast Burgers with Avocado Buns

Ingredients:
1 ripe avocado

1 egg, pasture-raised

1 red onion slice

1 tomato slice

1 lettuce leaf

Sesame seed for garnish

salt to taste

Directions:

Slice the avocado into half. It will serve as the bun.
Set aside.

Grease a skillet over medium flame and fry the egg
sunny-side up for 5 minutes or until set.

Assemble the breakfast burger by placing on top of
one avocado half with the egg, red onion, tomato,
and lettuce leaf. Top with the remaining avocado
bun.

Garnish with sesame seeds on top and season with
salt to taste.

Spinach Mushroom Omelet

Ingredients:

Olive oil, one tablespoon + one tablespoon

Spinach, fresh, chopped, one- and one-half cup

Green onion, one diced

Eggs, three

Feta cheese, one ounce

Mushrooms, button, five sliced

Red onion, diced, one quarter cup

Directions:

Sauté the mushrooms, onions, and spinach for three minutes in one tablespoon of olive oil and set to the side. Beat the eggs well and cook them in the other tablespoon of olive oil for three to four minutes until edges begin to brown. Sprinkle all the other ingredients onto half of the omelet and fold the other half over the sautéed ingredients. Cook for one minute on each side.

Weekend Breakfast Salad

Ingredients:
Eggs, four hard-boiled
Lemon, one
Arugula, ten cups
Quinoa, one cup cooked and cooled
Olive oil, two tablespoons
Dill, chopped, one half cup
Almonds, chopped, one cup
Avocado, one large sliced thin
Cucumber, chopped, one half cup
Tomato, one large cut in wedges

Directions:

Mix the quinoa, cucumber, tomatoes, and arugula. Toss these ingredients lightly together with olive oil, salt, and pepper. Transfer and arrange the egg and avocado on top. Top each salad with almonds and herbs. Drizzle with juice from the lemon.

Kale Turmeric Scramble

Ingredients:

Olive oil, two tablespoons

Kale, shredded, one half cup

Sprouts, one half cup

Garlic, minced, one tablespoon

Black pepper, one quarter teaspoon

Turmeric, ground, one tablespoon

Eggs, two

Directions:

Beat the eggs and add in the turmeric, black pepper, and garlic. Sauté the kale into the olive oil over medium heat for five minutes, and then pour this egg batter into the pan with the kale. Continue cooking, often stirring, until the eggs are cooked. Top with raw sprouts and serve.

Poached Salmon Egg Toast

Ingredients:

Bread, two slices rye or whole-grain toasted

Lemon juice, one quarter teaspoon

Avocado, two tablespoons mashed

Black pepper, one quarter teaspoon

Eggs, two poached

Salmon, smoked, four ounces

Scallions, one tablespoon sliced thin

Salt, one eighth teaspoon

Directions:

Add lemon juice to avocado with pepper and salt. Spread the mixed avocado over the toasted bread slices. Lay smoked salmon over toast and top with a poached egg. Top with sliced scallions.

Egg Muffins with Feta and Quinoa

Ingredients:

Eggs, eight

Tomatoes, chopped, one cup

Salt, one quarter teaspoon

Feta cheese, one cup

Quinoa, one cup cooked

Olive oil, two teaspoons

Oregano, fresh chop, one tablespoon

Black olives, chopped, one quarter cup

Onion, chopped, one quarter cup

Baby spinach, chopped, two cups

Directions:

Heat oven to 350. Spray oil a muffin pan with twelve cups. Cook spinach, oregano, olives, onion, and tomatoes for five minutes in the olive oil over medium heat. Beat eggs. Add the cooked mix of veggies to the eggs with the cheese and salt. Spoon mixture into muffin cups. Bake thirty minutes. These will remain fresh in the fridge for two days. To eat, just wrap in a paper towel and warm in the microwave for thirty seconds.

Peaches with Honey Almond Ricotta

Ingredients:

Spread

Ricotta, skim milk, one cup

Honey, one teaspoon

Almonds, thin slices, one half cup

Almond extract, one quarter teaspoon

To Serve

Peaches, sliced, one cup

Bread, whole grain bagel or toast

Directions:

Mix the almond extract, honey, ricotta, and almonds. Spread one tablespoon of this mix on toasted bread and cover with peaches.

Quinoa Breakfast Bowl

Ingredients:

Quinoa, two cups cooked

Eggs, twelve

Greek yogurt, plain, one quarter cup

Salt, one half teaspoon

Feta cheese, one cup

Cherry tomatoes, one pint cut in halves

Black pepper, one teaspoon

Garlic, minced, one teaspoon

Baby spinach, chopped, one cup

Olive oil, one teaspoon

Directions:

Mix the eggs, salt, pepper, garlic, onion powder, and yogurt. Cook the spinach and tomatoes for five minutes in the olive oil over medium heat. Pour in the egg mix and stir until eggs have set to your preferred doneness. Mix in quinoa and feta until they are hot. It will store in the fridge for two to three days.

Cream Cheese Salmon Toast

Ingredients:

Whole grain or rye toast, two slices

Red onion, chopped fine, two tablespoons

Cream cheese, low fat, two tablespoons

Basil flakes, one half teaspoon

Arugula or spinach, chopped, one half cup

Smoked salmon, two ounces

Directions:

Toast the wheat bread. Mix cream cheese and basil and spread this mixture on the toast. Add salmon, arugula, and onion.

Carrot Cake Overnight Oats

Ingredients:

Coconut or almond milk, one cup

Chia seeds, one tablespoon

Cinnamon, ground, one teaspoon

Raisins, one half cup

Cream cheese, low fat, two tablespoons at room temperature

Carrot, one large peel, and shred

Honey, two tablespoons

Vanilla, one teaspoon

Directions:

Mix all of the listed items and store them in a safe refrigerator container overnight. Eat cold in the morning. If you choose to warm this, just microwave for one minute and stir well before eating.

Cream Cheese Salmon Toast

Ingredients:

Whole grain or rye toast, two slices

Red onion, chopped fine, two tablespoons

Cream cheese, low fat, two tablespoons

Basil flakes, one half teaspoon

Arugula or spinach, chopped, one half cup

Smoked salmon, two ounces

Directions:

Toast the wheat bread. Mix cream cheese and basil and spread this mixture on the toast. Add salmon, arugula, and onion.

Carrot Cake Overnight Oats

Ingredients:

Coconut or almond milk, one cup

Chia seeds, one tablespoon

Cinnamon, ground, one teaspoon

Raisins, one half cup

Cream cheese, low fat, two tablespoons at room temperature

Carrot, one large peel, and shred

Honey, two tablespoons

Vanilla, one teaspoon

Directions:

Mix all of the listed items and store them in a safe refrigerator container overnight. Eat cold in the morning. If you choose to warm this, just microwave for one minute and stir well before eating.

Kiwi Strawberry Smoothie

Ingredients:

Kiwi, peeled and chopped, one

Strawberries, fresh or frozen, one-half cup chopped

Milk, almond or coconut, one cup

Basil, ground, one teaspoon

Turmeric, one teaspoon

Banana, diced, one

Chia seed powder, one quarter cup

Directions:

Drink immediately after all the ingredients have been well mixed.

Mediterranean Frittata

Ingredients:

Eggs, six

Feta cheese, crumbled, one quarter cup

Black pepper, one quarter teaspoon

Oil, spray, or olive

Oregano, one teaspoon

Milk, almond or coconut, one quarter cup

Sea salt, one teaspoon

Black olives, chopped, one quarter cup

Green olives, chopped, one quarter cup

Tomatoes, diced, one quarter cup

Directions:

Heat oven to 400. Oil one eight by eight-inch baking dish. Combine the milk into the eggs, and then add other ingredients. Pour all of this mixture into the baking dish and bake for twenty minutes.

Maple Oatmeal

Ingredients:

Maple flavoring, one teaspoon

Cinnamon, one teaspoon

Sunflower seeds, three tablespoons

Pecans, one-half cup chopped

Coconut flakes, unsweetened, one quarter cup

Walnuts, one-half cup chopped

Milk, almond or coconut, one half cup

Chia seeds, four tablespoons

Directions:

Pulse the sunflower seeds, walnuts, and pecans in a food processor to crumble. Or you can just put the nuts in a sturdy plastic bag, wrap the bag with a towel, lay it on a sturdy surface, and beat the towel with a hammer until the nuts are crumbled. Mix the crushed nuts with the rest of the ingredients and pour them into a large pot. Simmer this mixture over low heat for thirty minutes. Stir often, so the mix does not stick to the bottom. Serve garnished with fresh fruit or a sprinkle of cinnamon if desired.

Tomato Omelet

Ingredients:

Eggs, two

Basil, fresh, one half cup

Cherry tomatoes, one half cup

Black pepper, one teaspoon

Cheese, any type, one-quarter cup shredded

Salt, one half teaspoon

Olive oil, two tablespoons

Directions:

Cut the tomatoes into quarters. Fry it in the olive oil for three minutes. Set the tomatoes off to the side. Put salt and pepper to the eggs in a small bowl and beat together well. Pour the beaten egg mixture into the pan and use a spatula to gently work around the edges under the omelet, letting the eggs fry unmoved for three minutes. When the center third of the egg mix is still runny, add on the basil, tomatoes, and cheese. Fold over half of the omelet onto the other half. Cook two more minutes and serve.

Chia Breakfast Pudding

Ingredients:

Chia seeds, four tablespoons

Almond butter, one tablespoon

Coconut milk, three-fourths cup

Cinnamon, one teaspoon

Vanilla, one teaspoon

Cold coffee, three-fourths cup

Directions:

Combine all of the fixings well and pour them into a refrigerator-safe container. Cover well and let refrigerate overnight.

Slow Cooker French toast Casserole

Ingredients:

2 eggs

2 egg whites

1 ½ almond milk or 1% milk

2 tbsp raw honey

1/2 tsp cinnamon

1 tsp vanilla extract

9 slices bread

For filling:

3cups apples (diced)

2 tbsp raw honey

1 tbsp lemon juice

1/2 tsp cinnamon

1/3 cup of pecans

Directions:

Put the first six items into a bowl and mix.

Grease the slow cooker with a non-stick cooking spray.

Combine all the ingredients of the filling in a small bowl and set aside. Coat the apple pieces into the filling properly.

Cut slices of bread in half (triangle), then place three apple slices on the bottom and some filing over. Layer the bread slices and filling in the same pattern.

Put the egg batter on the layers of bread and filling. Set the cooker on high heat for 2 ½ hours or low heat for 4 hours.

Crackpot Banana Foster

Ingredients:

1 tbsp melted coconut oil (unrefined)

3 tbsp honey

1/4 tsp cinnamon

Juice of ½ medium-sized lemon

5 bananas (medium-sized)

For Garnish:

Chopped nuts

Greek Yogurt

Directions:

Put the first four items in the slow cooker and mix.

Cut the bananas in half and toss into the mixture inside the slow cooker.

Set on the cooker on low heat for 1 ½ to 2 hours.

Serve with chopped nuts or plain Greek yogurt.

Chicken and Quinoa Burrito Bowl

Ingredients:

1 lb. chicken thighs (skinless, boneless)

1 cup of chicken broth

1 can have diced tomatoes (14.50z)

1 onion (chopped)

3 cloves garlic (chopped)

2 tsp chili powder

½ tsp coriander

½ tsp garlic powder

1 bell pepper (finely chopped)

15oz pinto beans (drained)

1 ½ cup cheddar cheese (grated)

Directions:

Combine chicken, tomatoes, broth, onion, garlic, chili powder, garlic powder, coriander, and salt. Set the cooker on low heat.

Remove the chicken, and shred into pieces with a fork and knife.

Put the chicken back in the slow cooker and add quinoa and pinto beans.

Set the cooker on low heat for 2 hours.

Add cheese on to the top and continue to cook and stir gently until the cheese melts.

Serve.

Nutty Blueberry Banana Oatmeal

Ingredients:

2 cup rolled eats

1/4 cup almonds (toasted)

1/4 cup walnuts

1/4 cup pecans

2 tbsp ground flax seeds

1 tsp ground ginger

1 tsp cinnamon

1/4 tsp sea salt

2 tbsp coconut sugar

½ tsp baking powder

2 cups of milk

2 bananas

1 cup fresh blueberries

1 tbsp maple syrup

1 tsp vanilla extract

1 tbsp melted butter

Yogurt for serving

Directions:

In a large bowl, add nuts, flax seeds, baking powder, spices, and coconut sugar and mix.

In another bowl, beat eggs, milk, maple syrup, and vanilla extract.

Slice the bananas in half and layer them in the slow cooker pot with blueberries.

Add oats mixture and pour the milk mixture on the top.

Drizzle with melted butter,

Cook the slow cooker on low heat for 4 hours or on high heat for 4 hours. Cook till the liquid is absorbed and oats are golden brown.

Serve warm and top it off with plain Greek yogurt.

Slow Cooker Steamed Cinnamon Apples

Ingredients:

8 apples (peeled, cored)

2 tsp lemon juice

2 tsp cinnamon

½ tsp nutmeg

¼ cup of coconut sugar

Directions:

Put all the items in the slow cooker pot.

Set the slow cooker pot on a low setting for 3 to 4 hours.

Cook till the apples are tender. Serve.

Carrot Rice with Scrambled Eggs

Ingredients:

For Sweet Tamari Soy Sauce

3 tbsp tamari sauce (gluten-free)

1 tbsp water

2-3 tbsp molasses

For Spicy Mix-ins

3 garlic cloves

1 small shallot (sliced)

2 long red chilies

Pinch of ground ginger

For the Carrot Rice:

2 Tbsp sesame oil

5 eggs

4 large carrots

8 ounces sausage (chicken or any type of – gluten-free and minced).

1 tbsp sweet soy sauce

1 cup bean sprouts

1/2 cup fined diced broccoli

salt and pepper to taste

For Garnish:

Cilantro

Asian chili sauce

Sesame seeds

Directions:

For the Sauce:

In a saucepan, boil molasses, water, and tamari at a high flame.

Lower the flame after the sauce boils and cook till molasses is completely dissolved.

Place the sauce in a separate bowl.

For the Carrot Rice:

In a bowl, combine ginger, garlic, onion, and red chilies.

To make rice out of the carrots, spiralize the carrots in a spiralizer.

Pulse the spiralized carrots in a food processor.

Cut broccoli into small dice like pieces

Add the sausage, carrots, broccoli, and the bean sprouts into the bowl of onion, ginger, garlic, and chilies.

Add the spicy mix of vegetables and the tamari sauce in the slow cooker pot.

Set the cooker on high heat for 3 hours or low heat for 6 hours.

Scramble two eggs in a non-stick frying pan or skillet.

Dish out the carrot rice and add scrambled eggs on top.

Garnish with sesame seeds, Asian chili sauce, and cilantro.

Conclusion

Ease into an anti-inflammatory eating pattern by gradually modifying your meals and snacks. That way, these changes can become a lifestyle change.

Make vegetables the focus of your meals; fill half your plate with cooked and/or raw vegetables.

Consider how often you eat red meat; aim for no more than twice a week.

To reduce red meat intake, add fish to your menu twice a week. Eat at least one plant-based meal each week featuring chickpeas, lentils or tofu, for example, and build from there.

Just one meal or snack or heck, even a weekend full of fried food cannot induce a state of "inflammation." However, an anti-inflammatory diet may help many people lose weight because it's chock-full of nutrient-dense and delicious foods.

Printed in Great Britain
by Amazon

25167405R00089